Color Your Cares Away

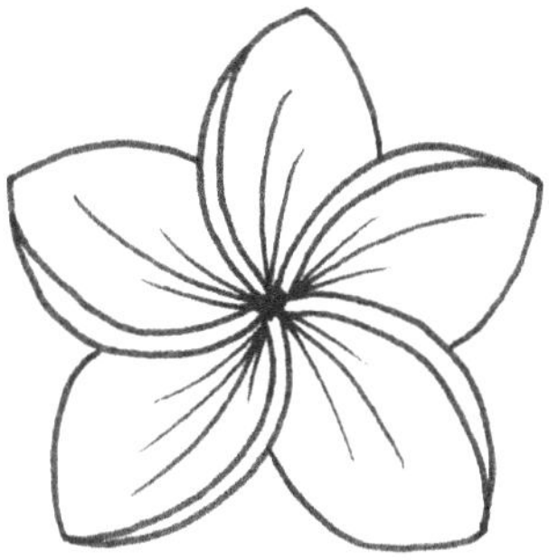

BY

Mellisa Hudell

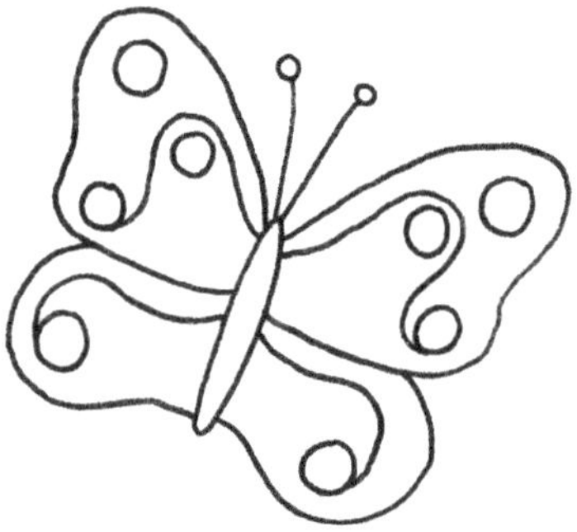

ISBN-13: 978-1-5186-5386-5

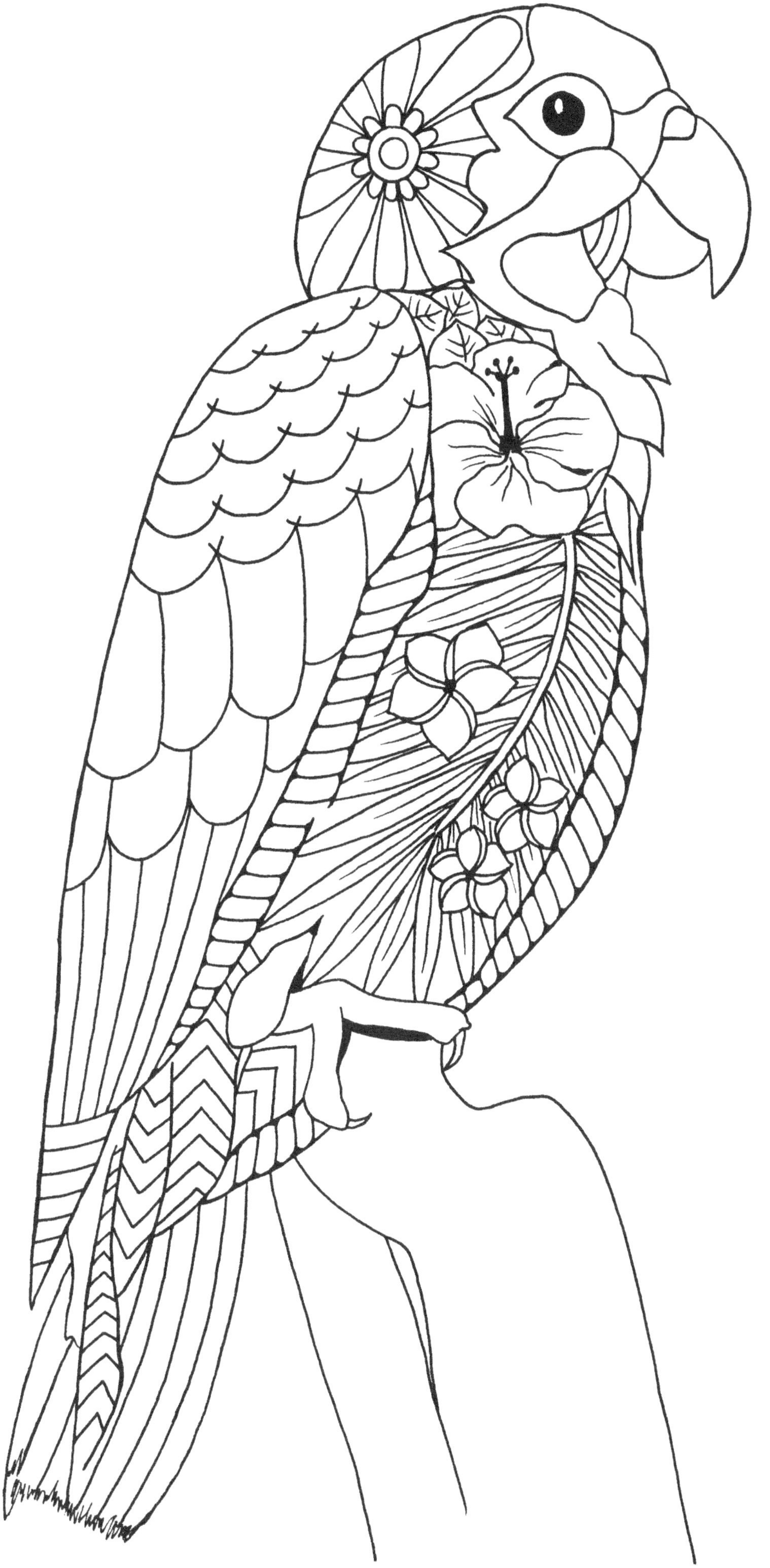

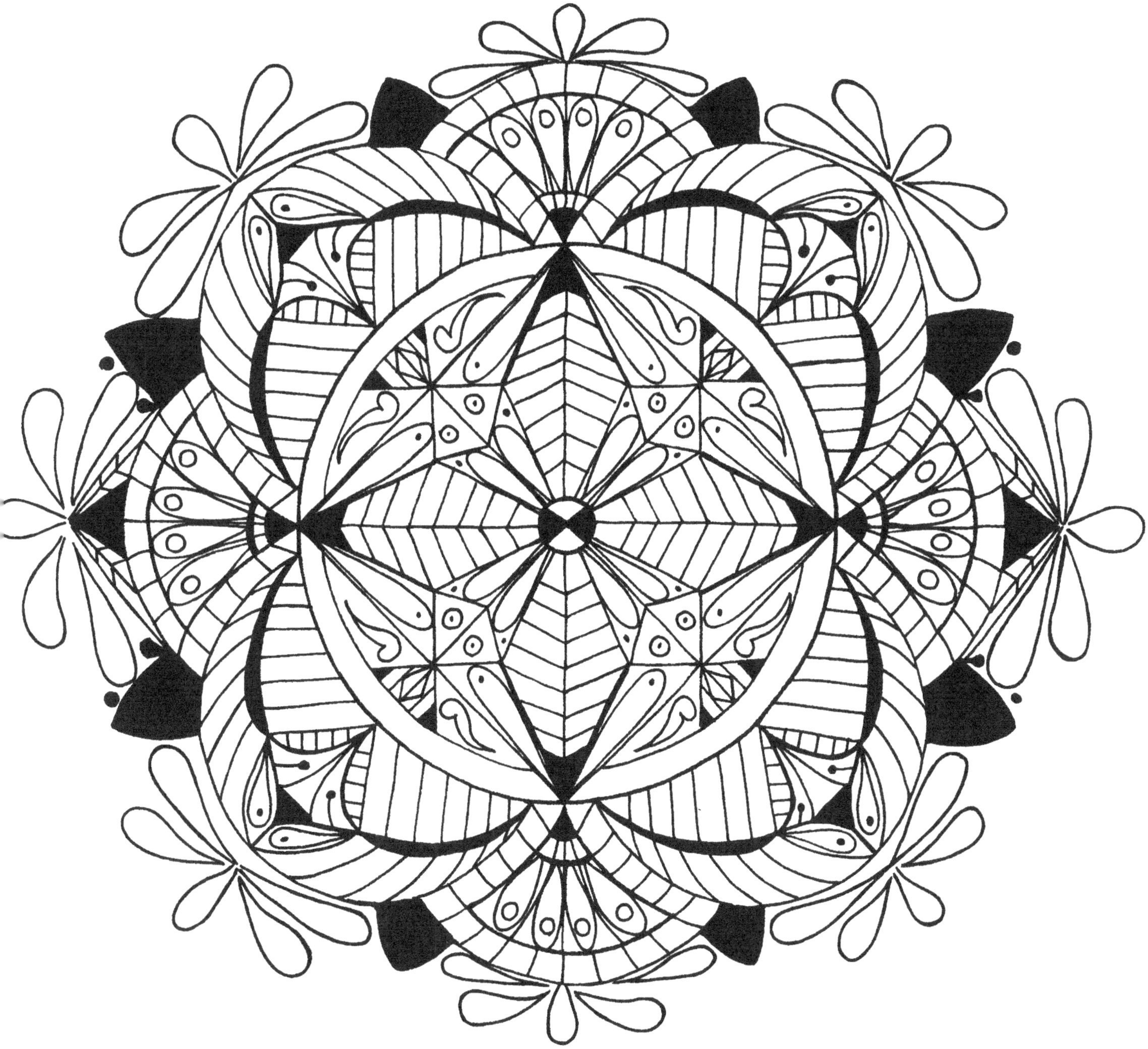

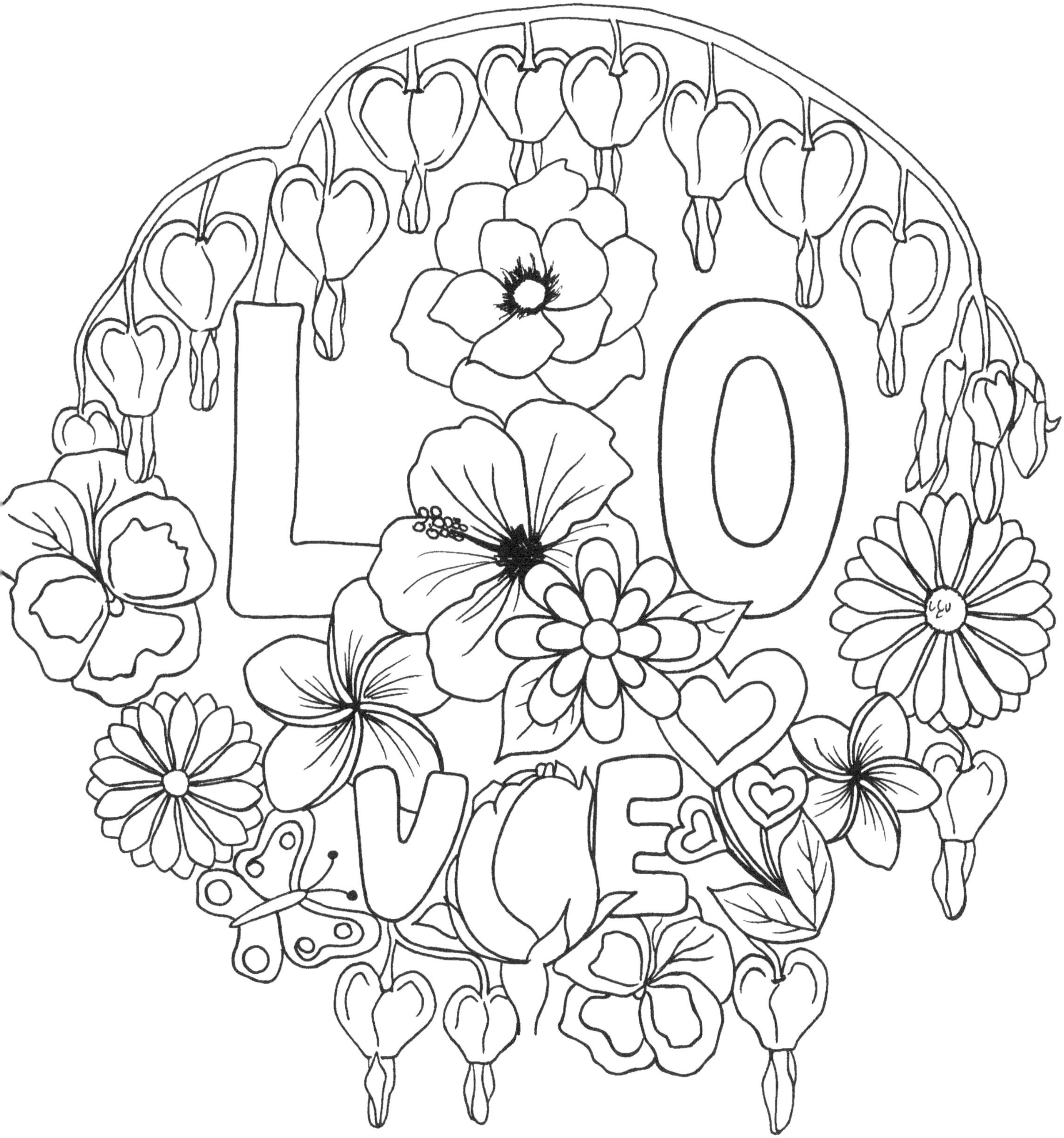
LOVE

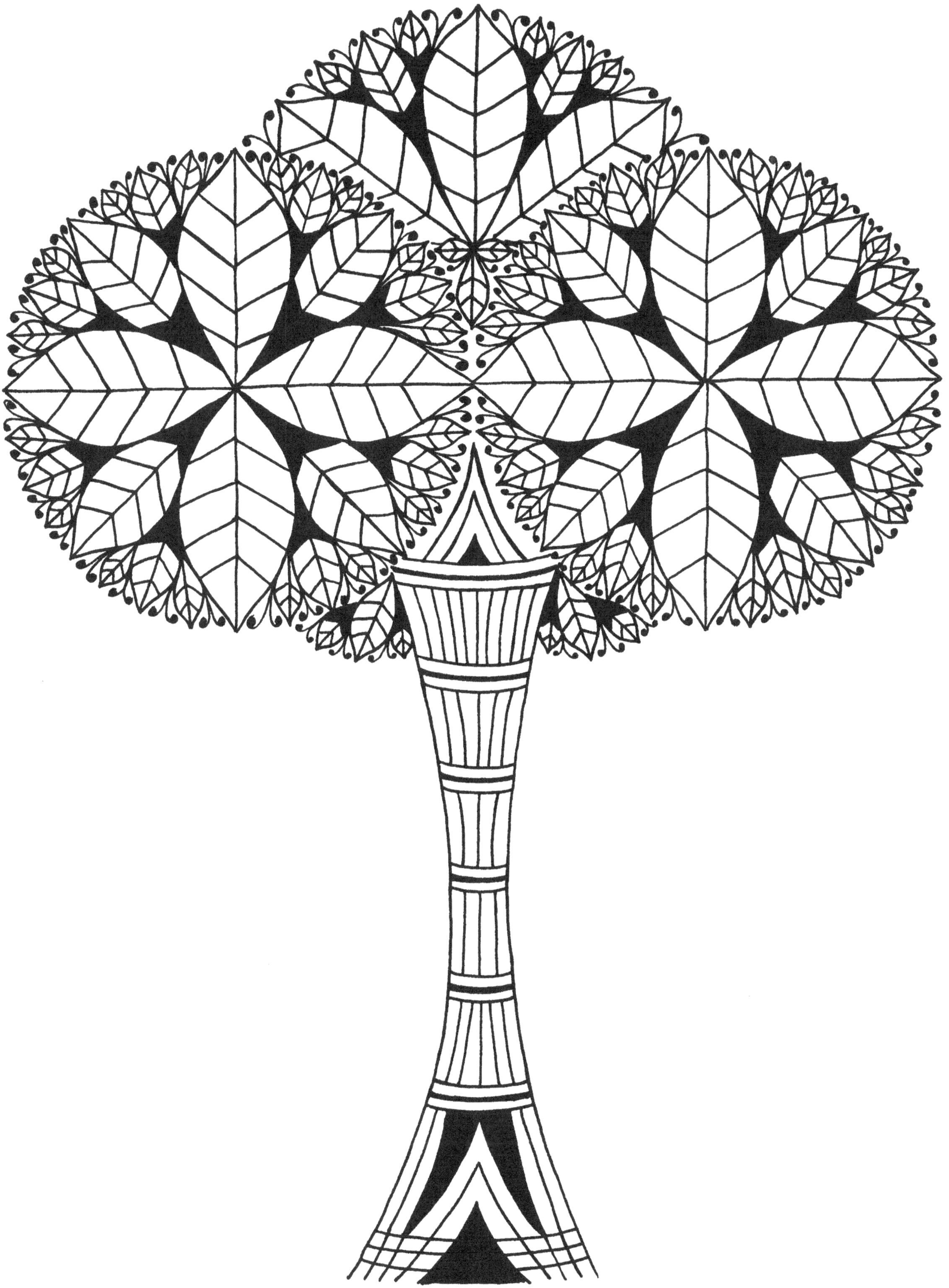

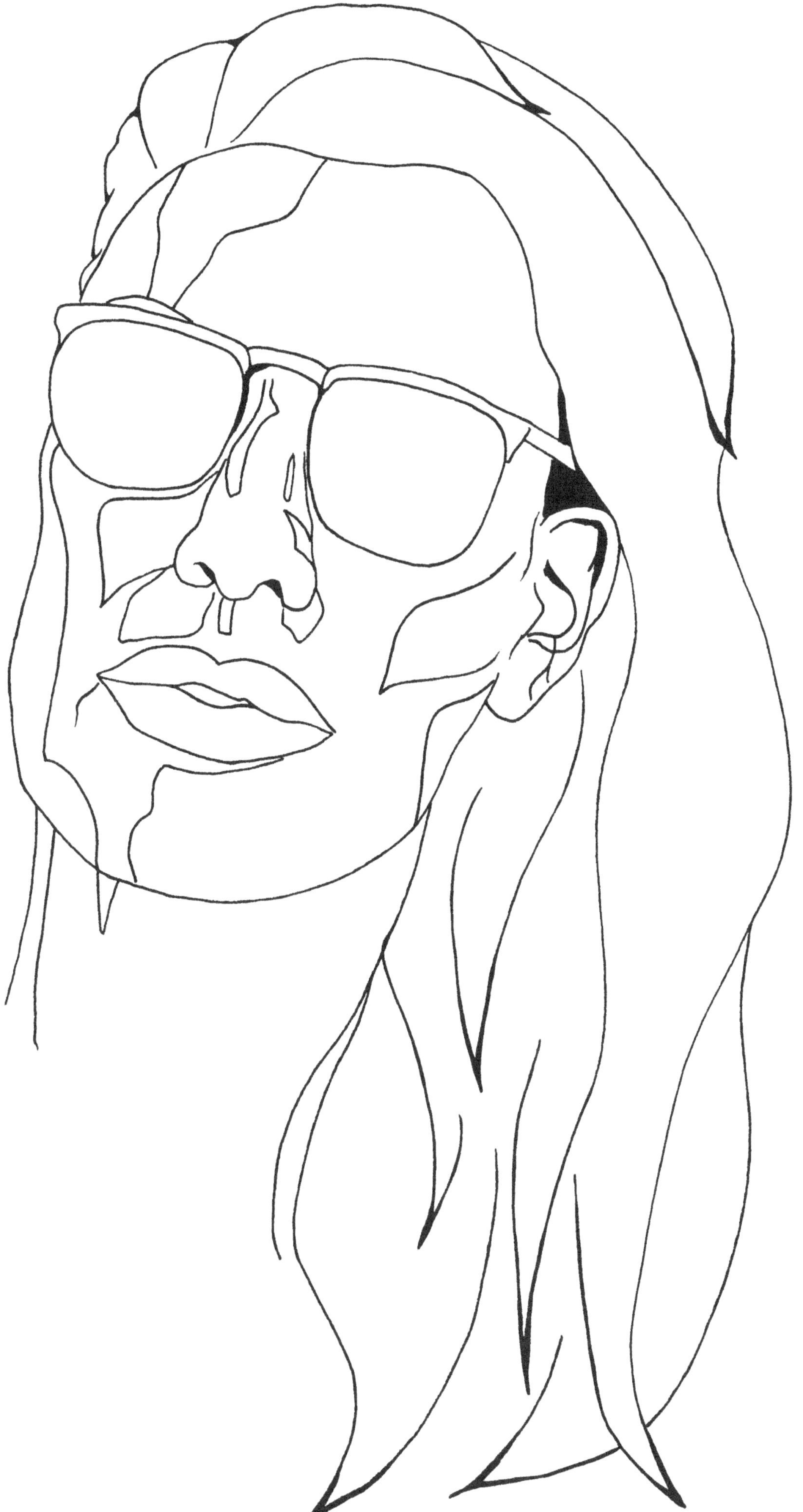

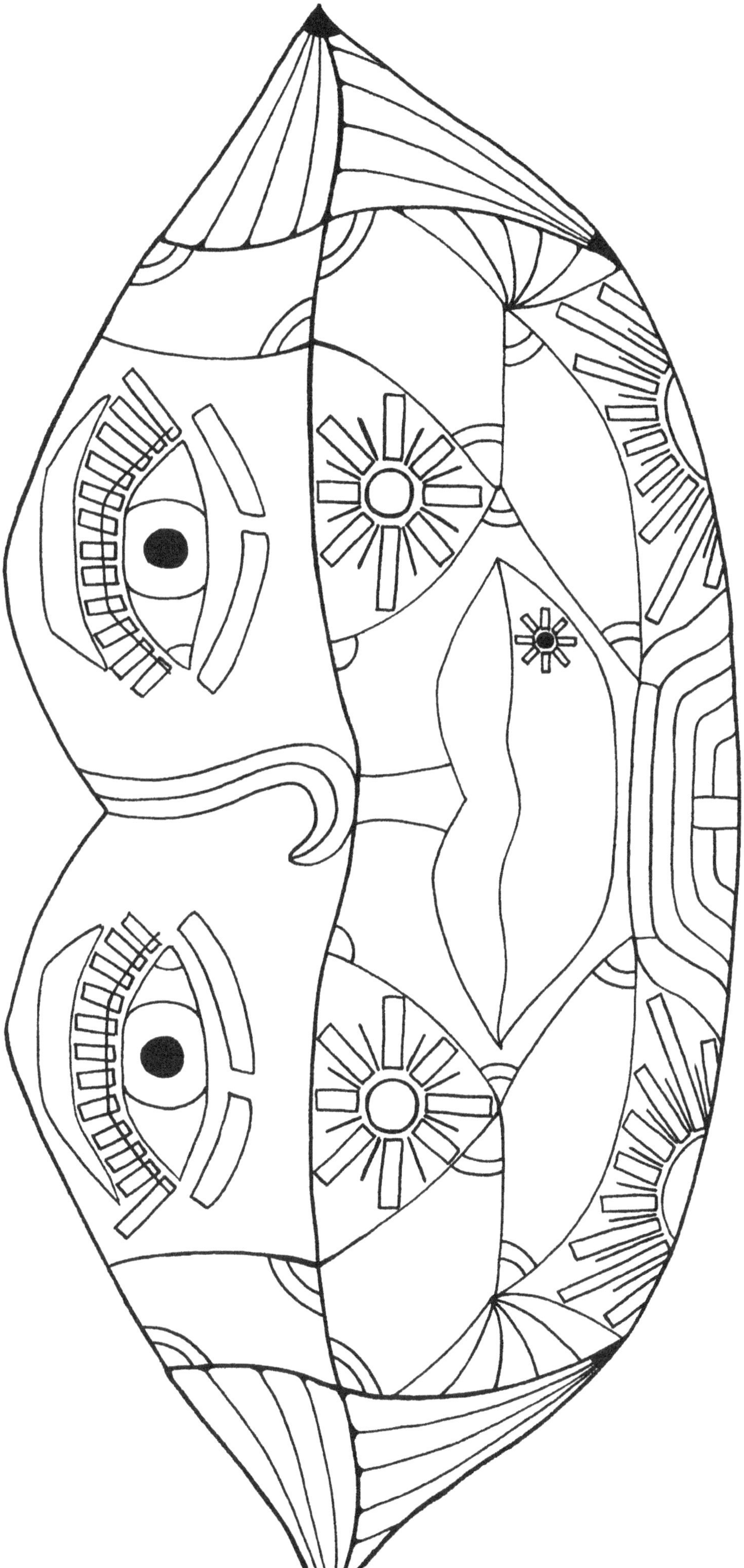

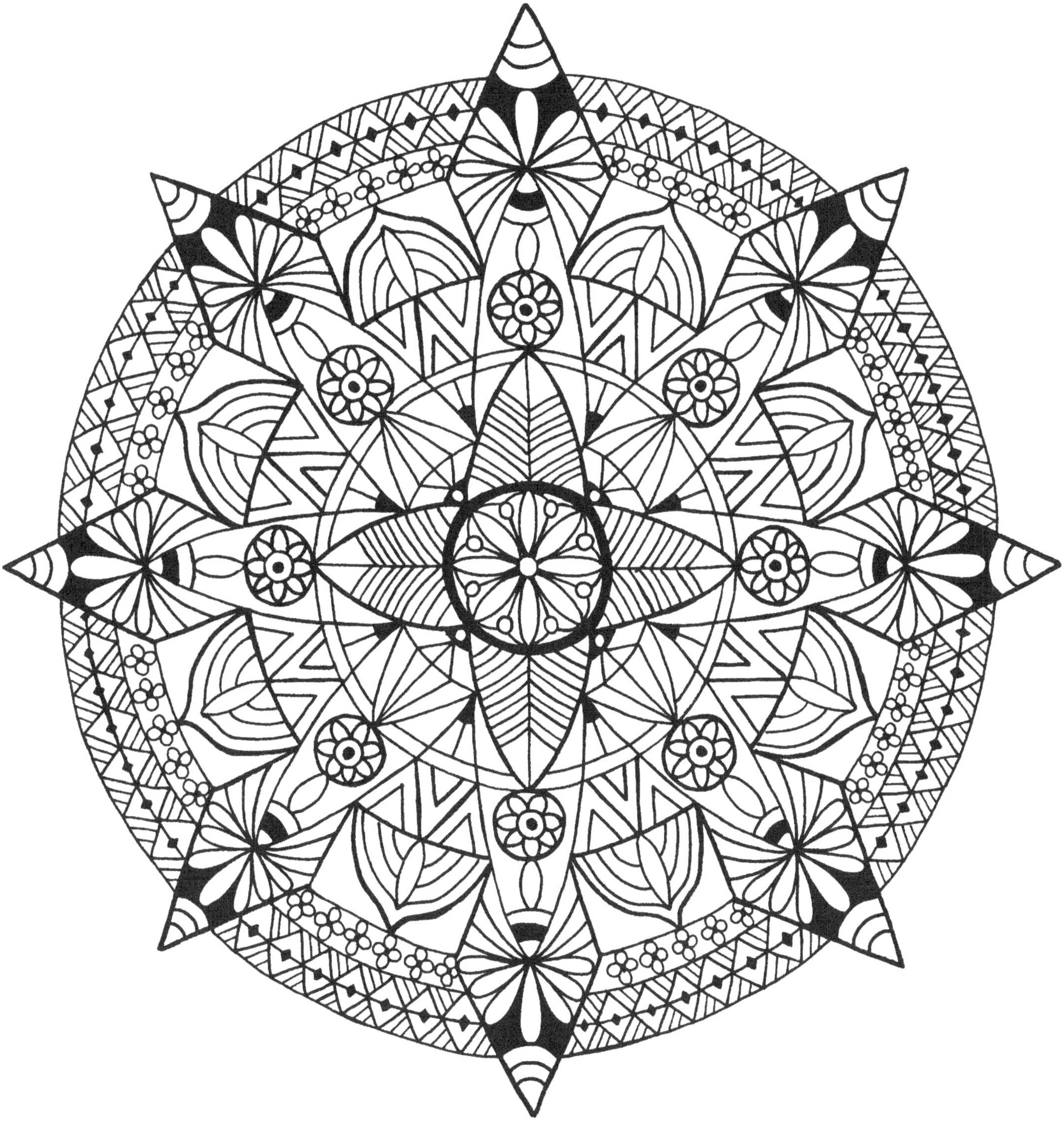

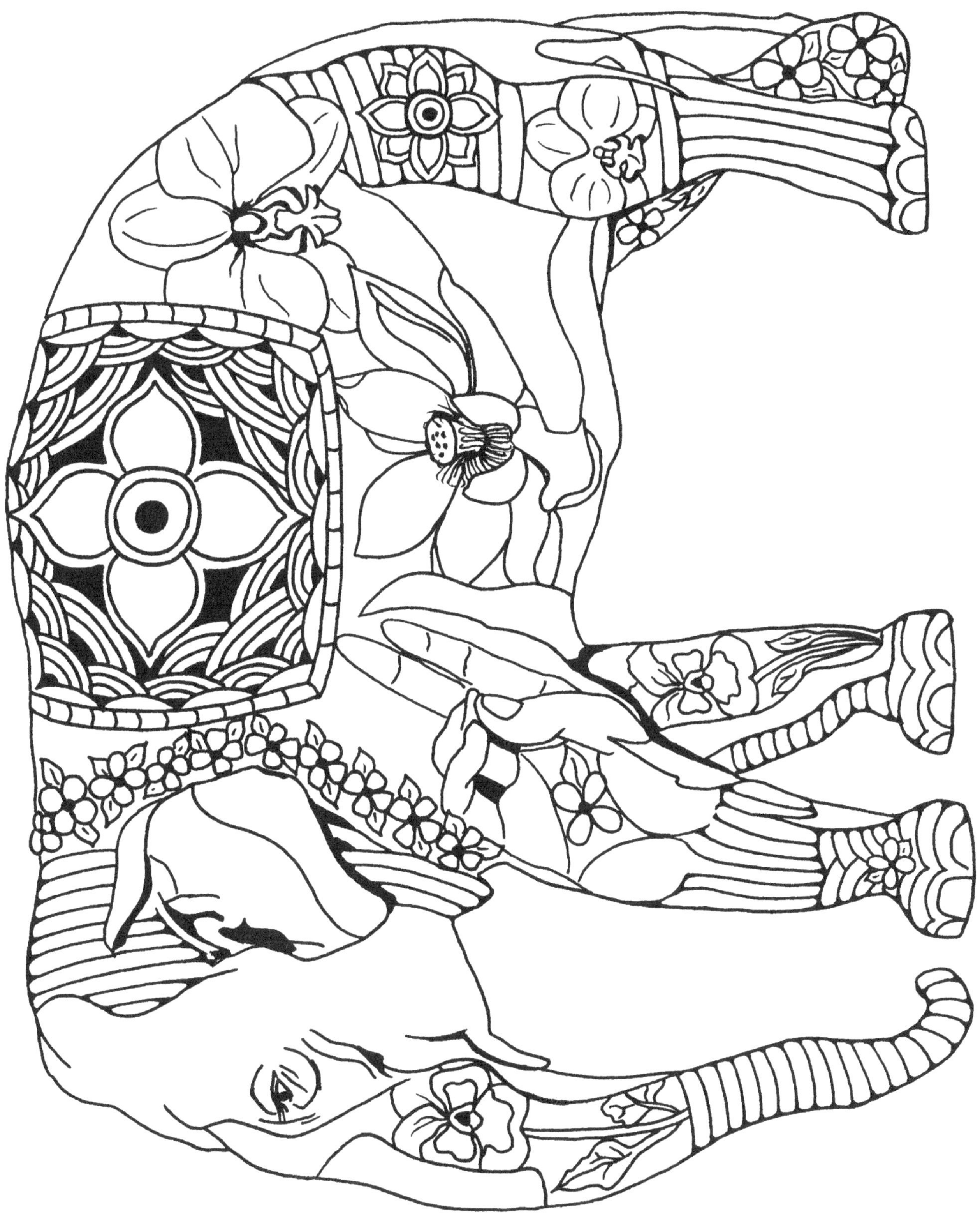

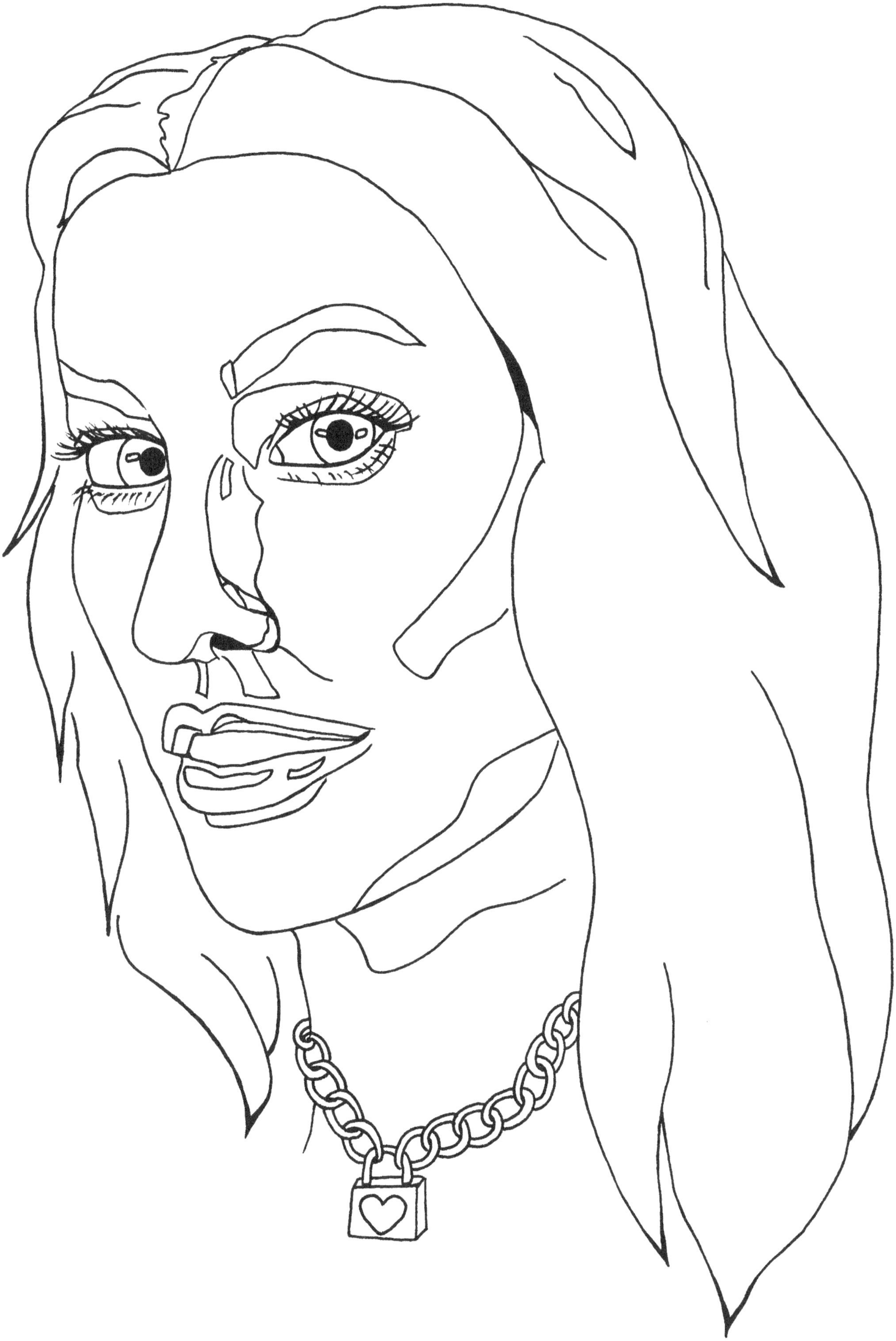

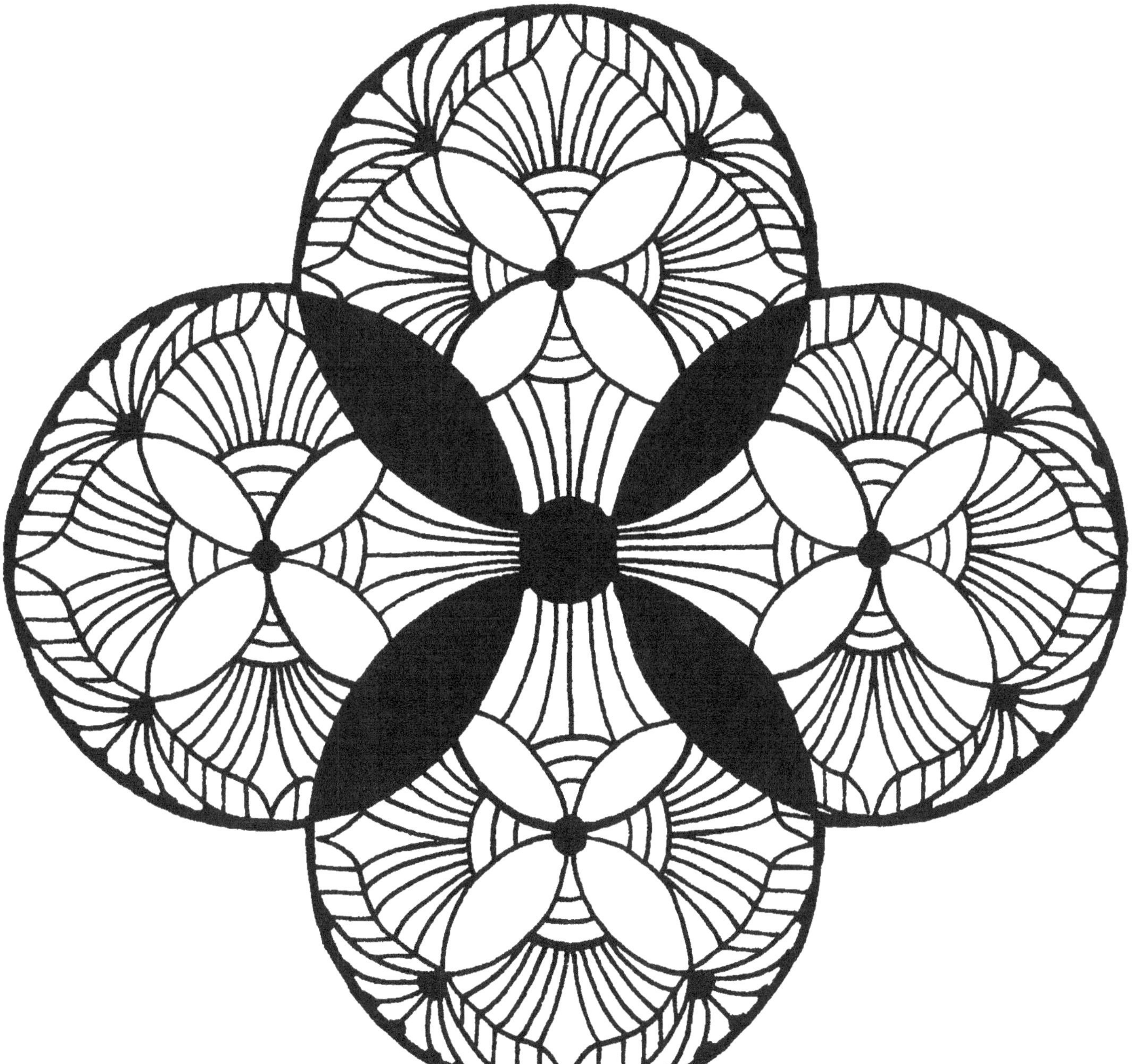

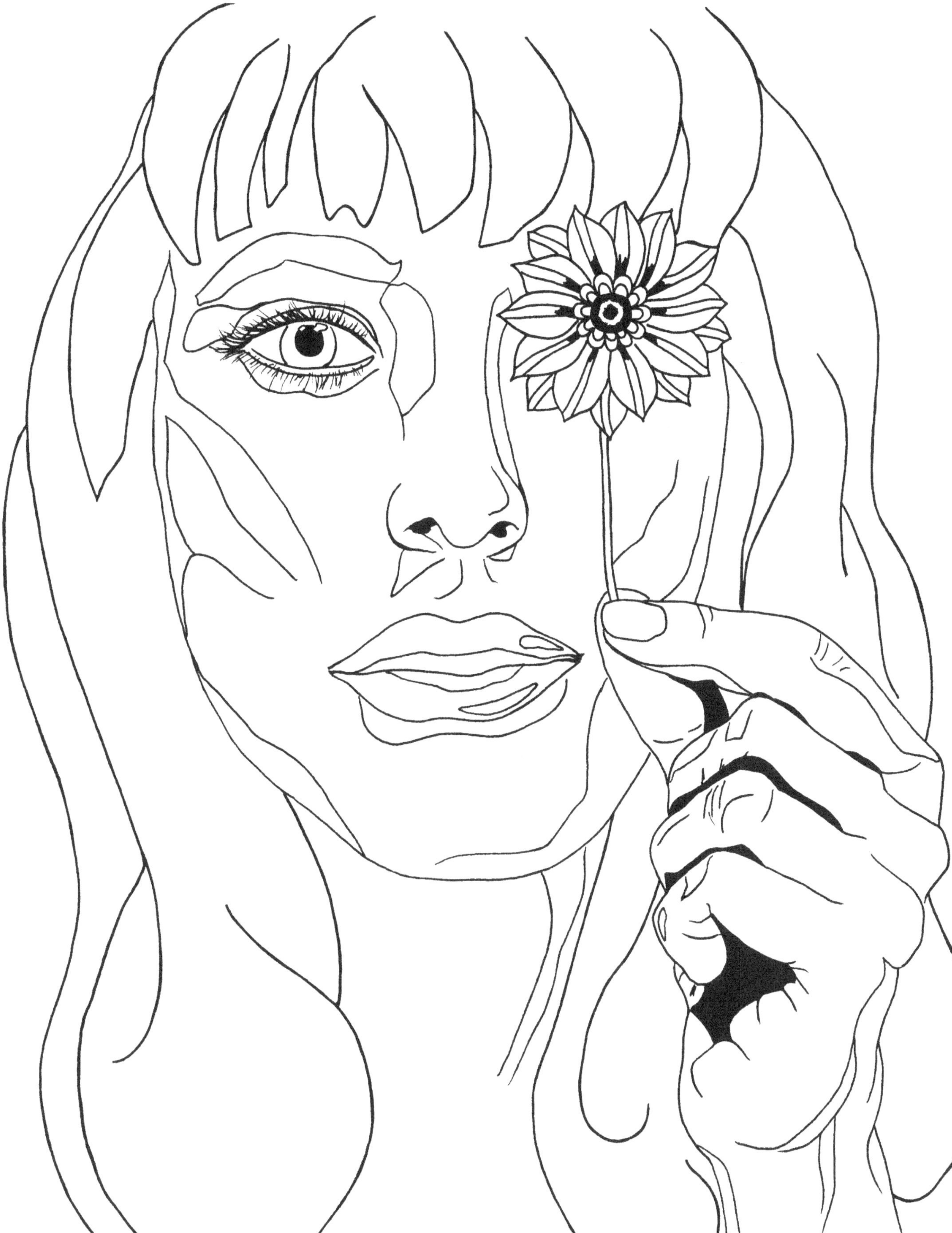

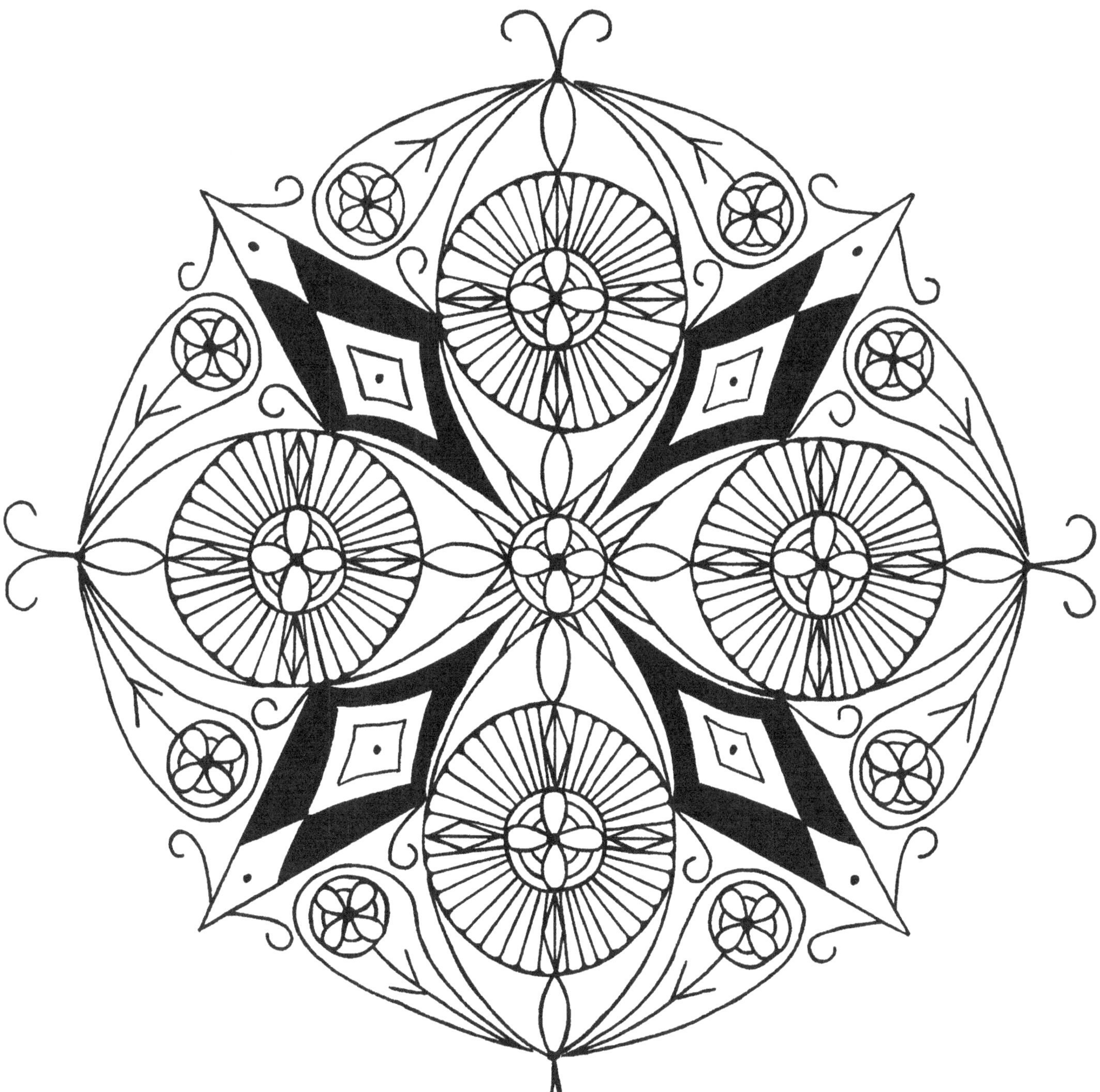

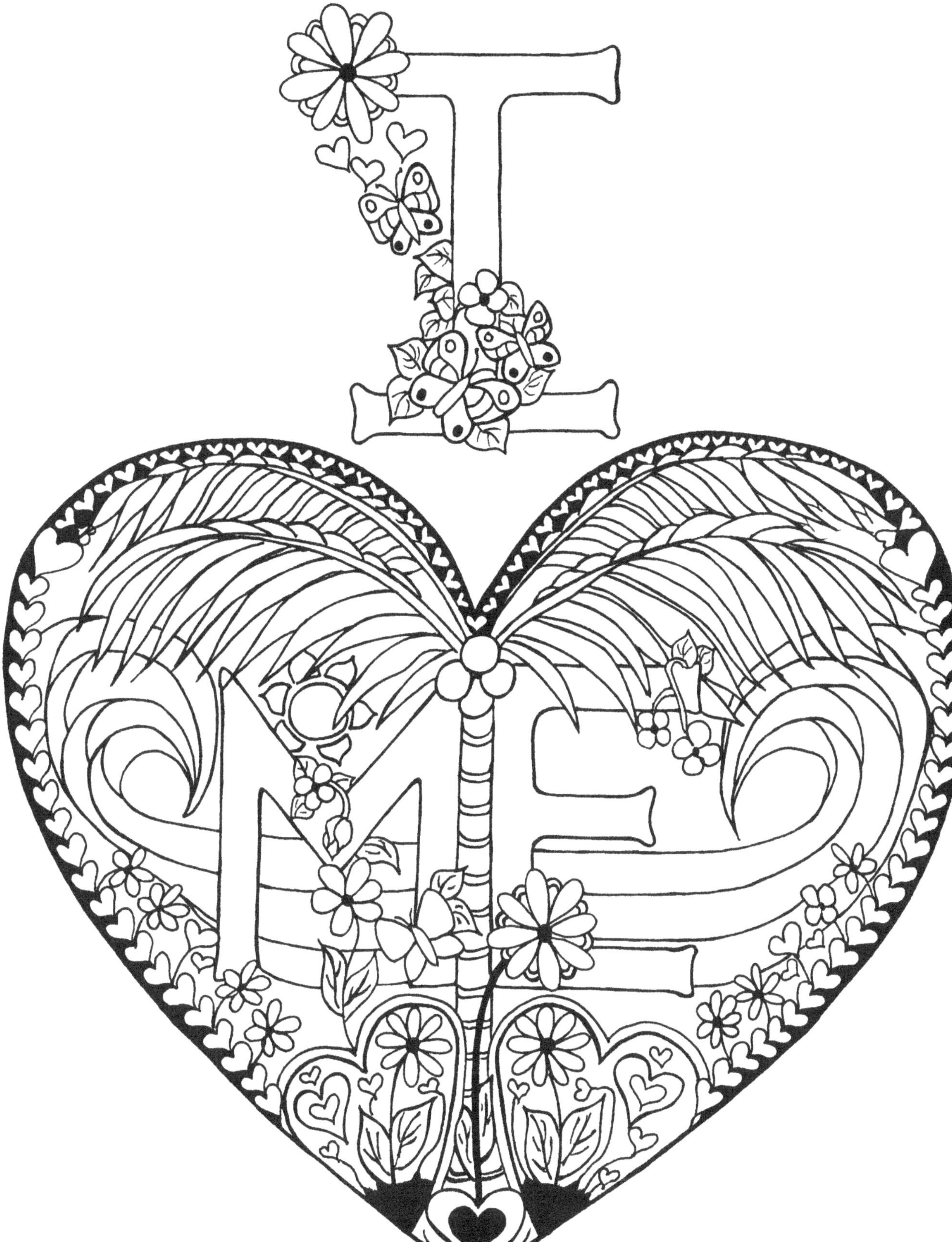
I
ME

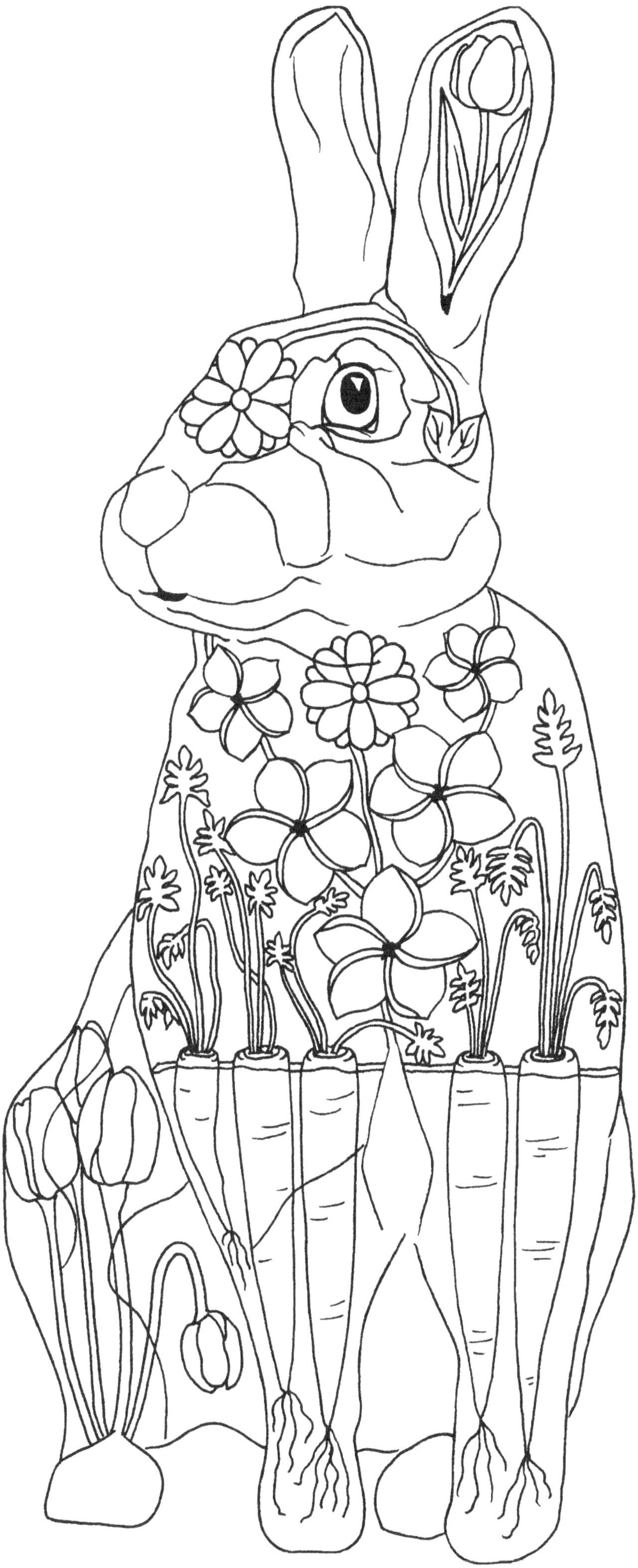

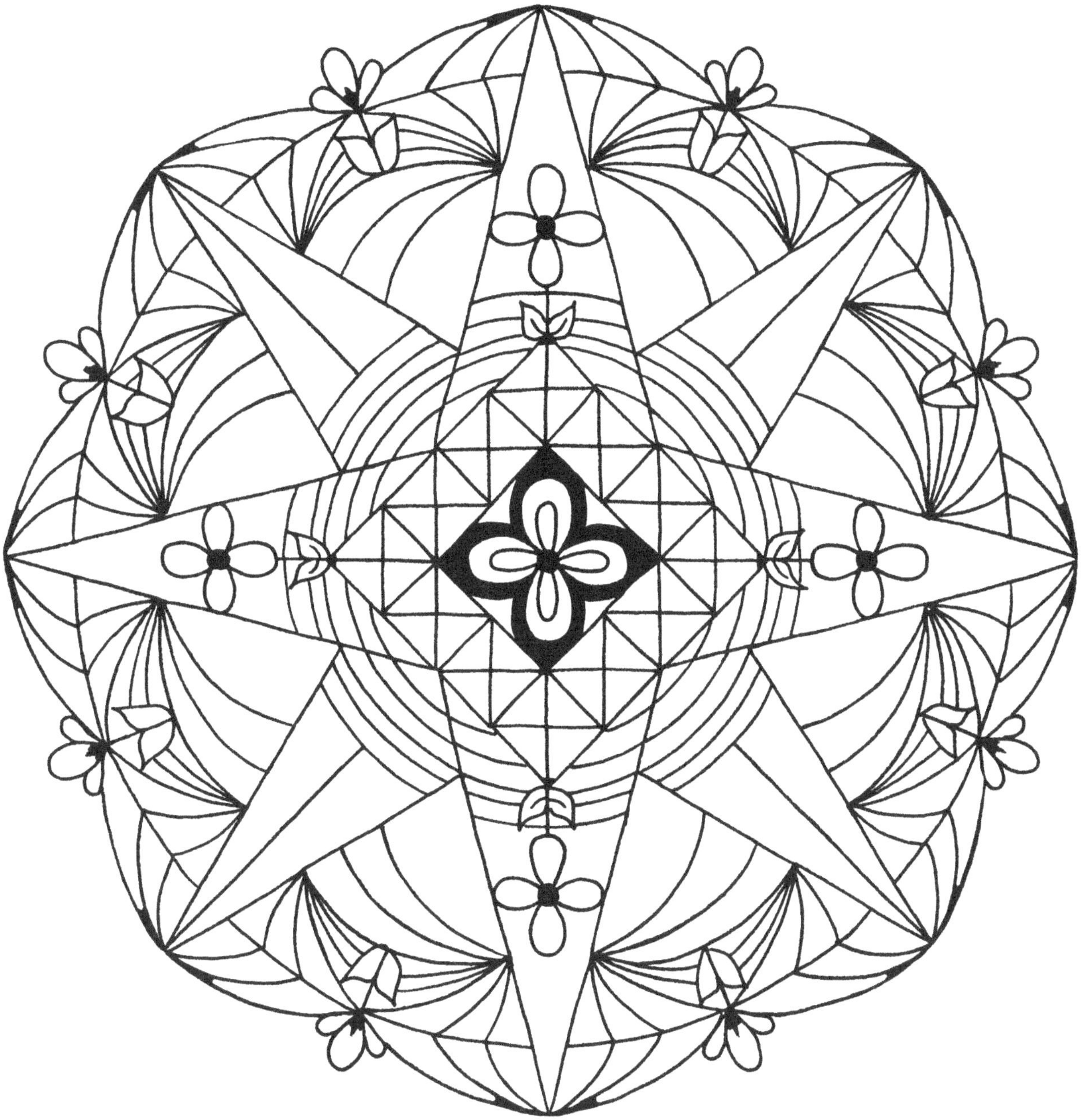

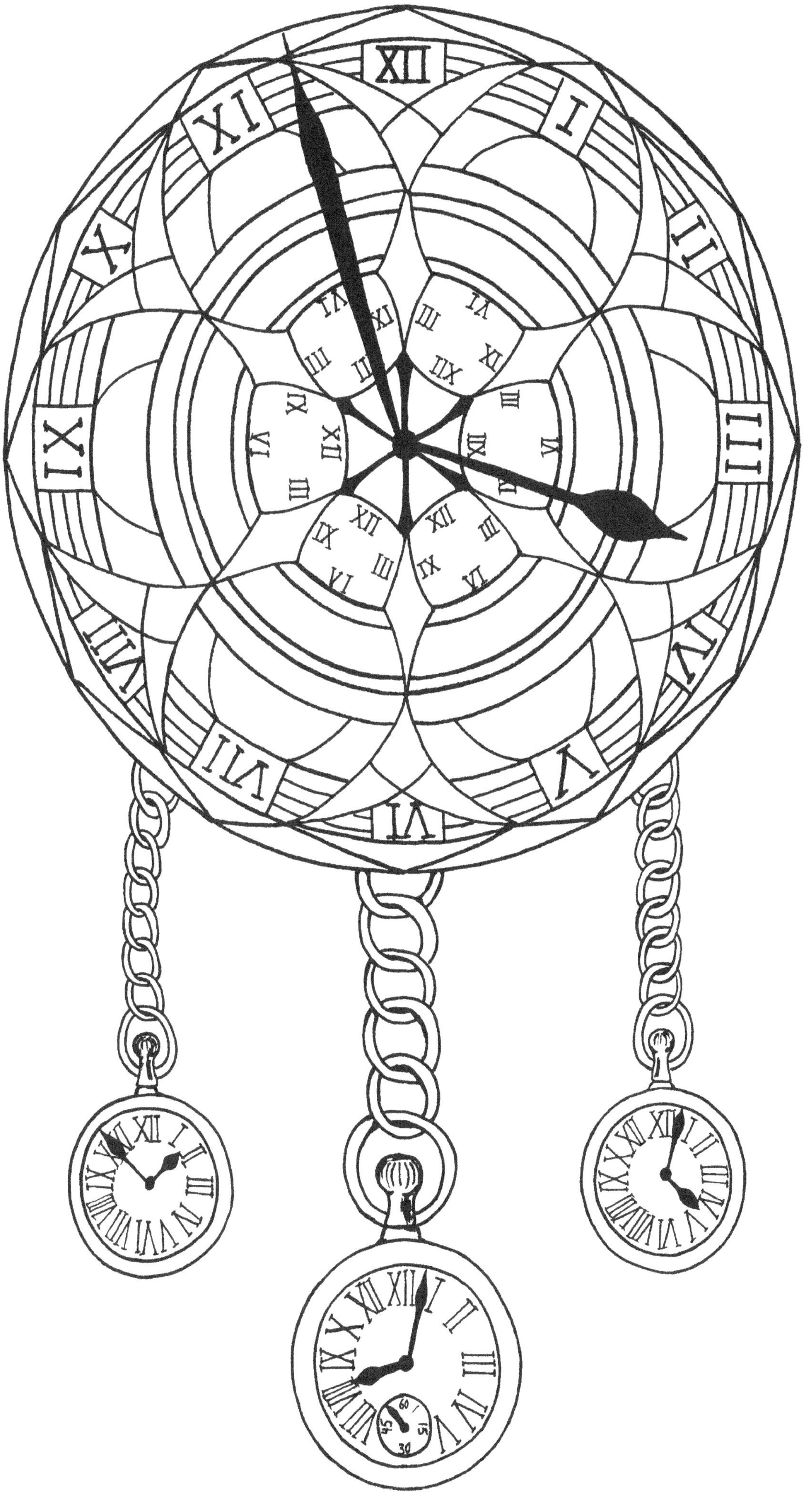

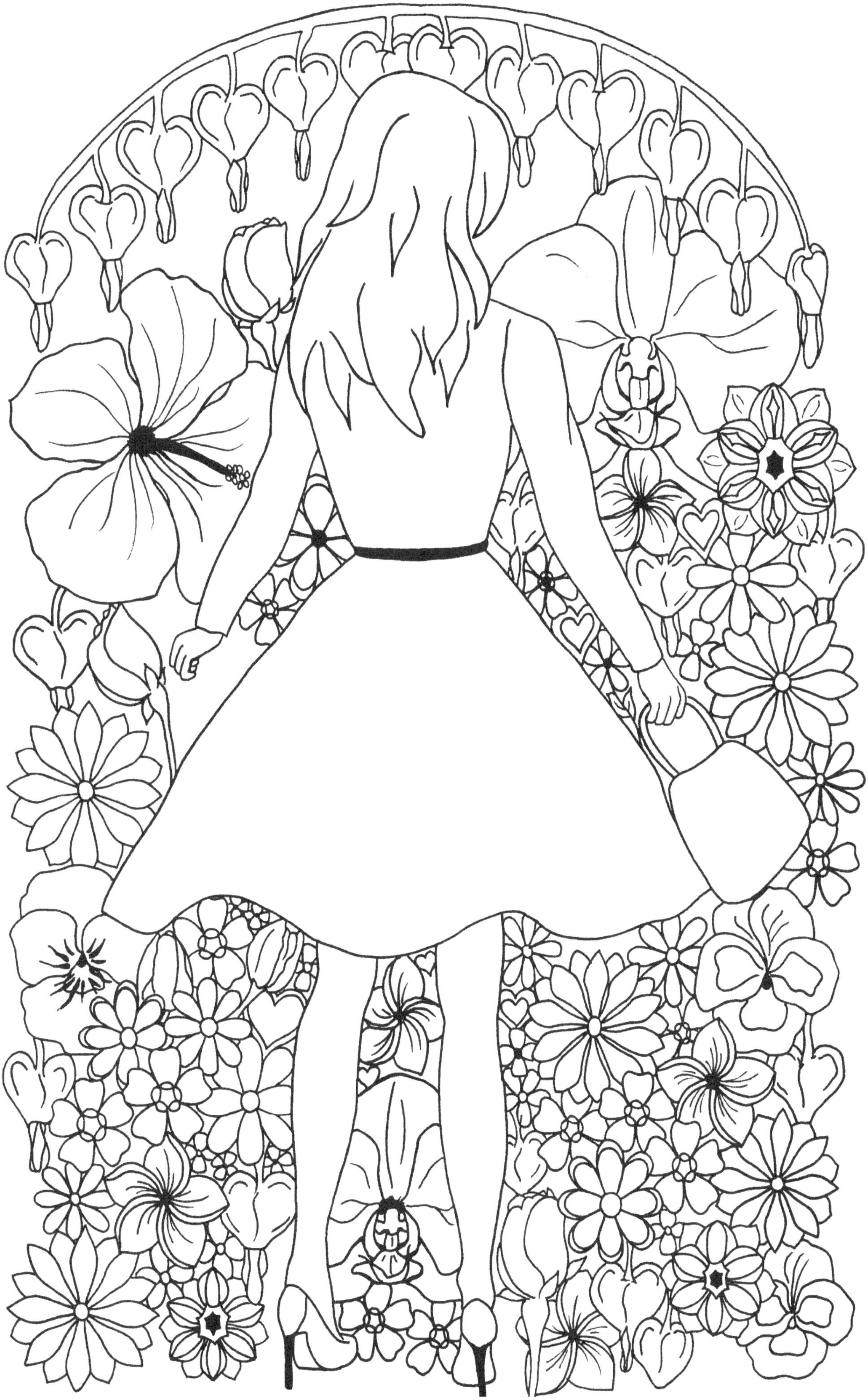

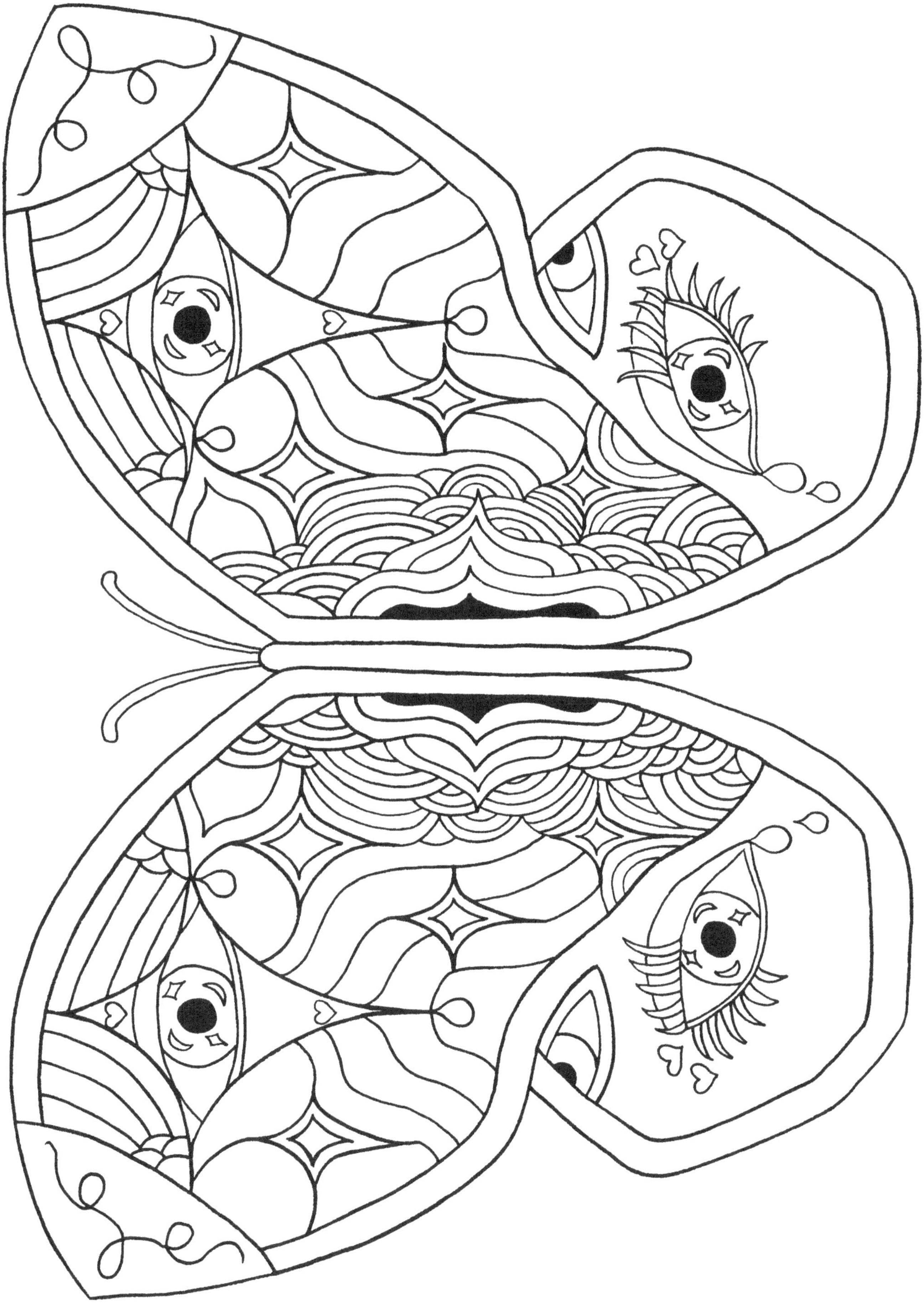

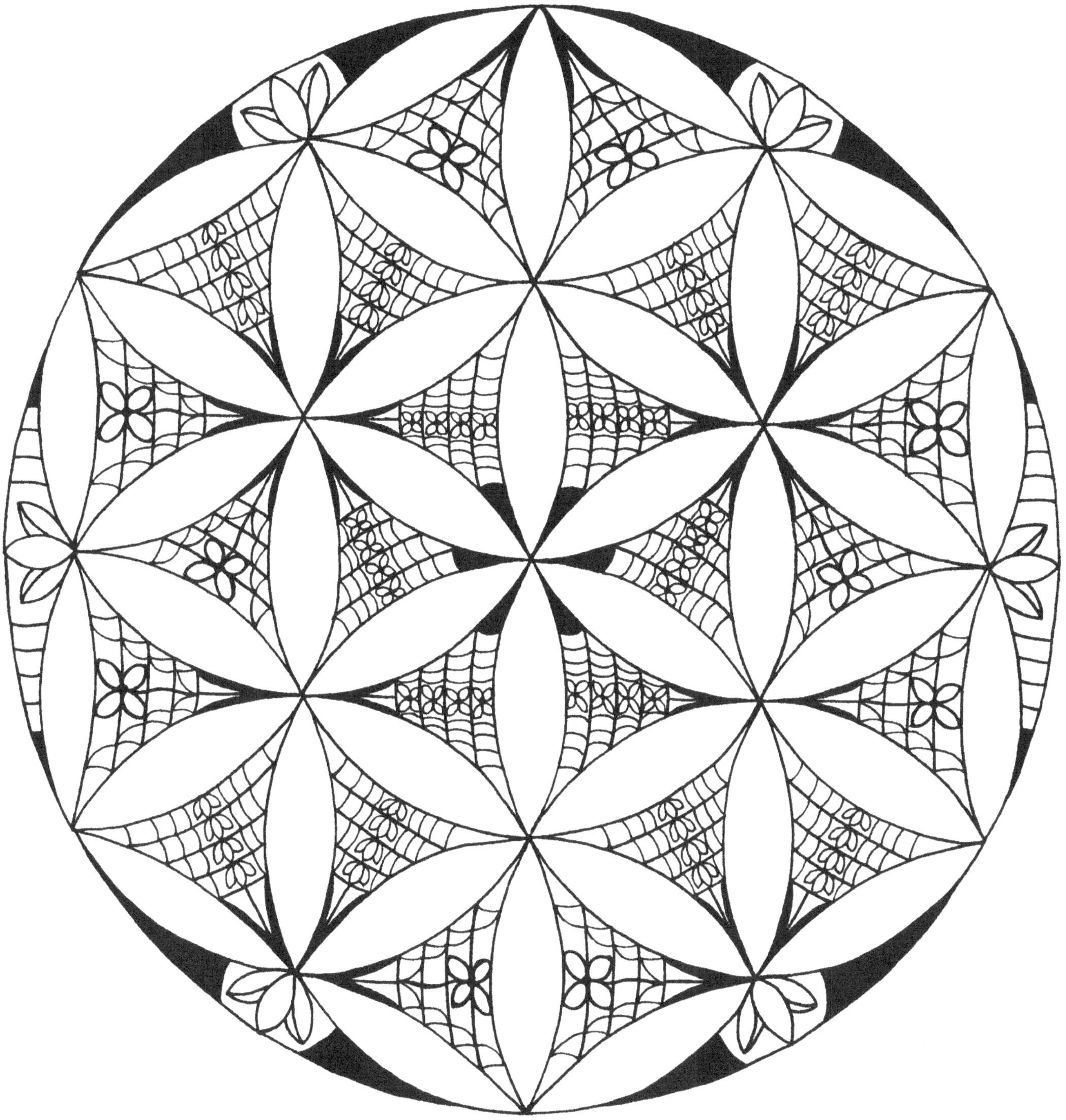

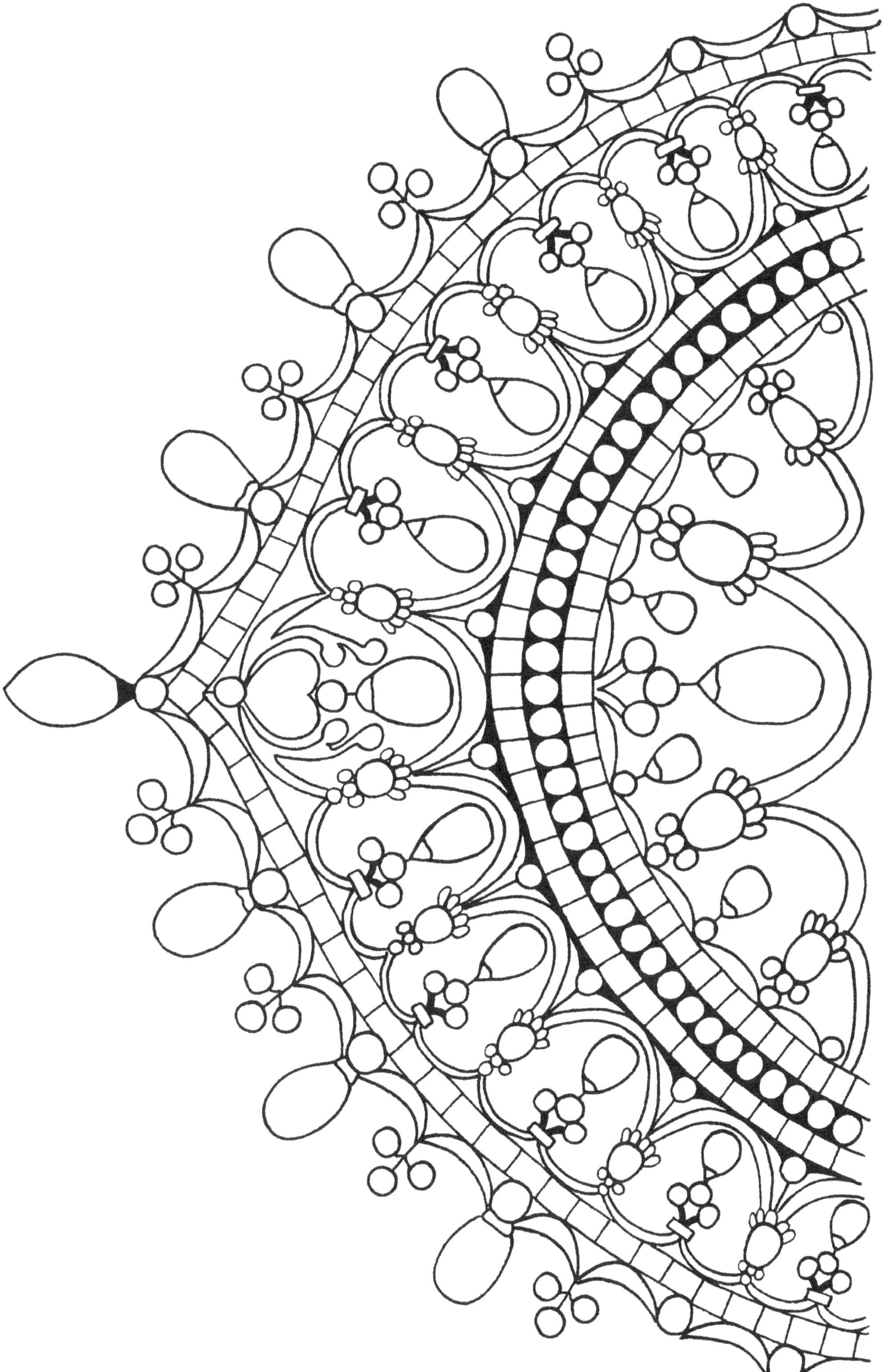

www.ingramcontent.com/pod-product-compliance
Lightning Source LLC
Chambersburg PA
CBHW080652180526
45168CB00008B/3396
* 9 7 8 1 5 1 8 6 5 3 8 6 5 *